Piano/Vocal

THE ACTOR'S SONGBOOK/ MEN'S EDITION

Character Songs, Comedy Songs,
Vaudeville Songs, Dramatic Songs, and Ballads for Audition and Performance

W9-BRG-702

ISBN 1-7935-2344-3

HAL•LEONARD™
CORPORATION
7777 W. BLUEMOUND RD. P.O. BOX 13819 MILWAUKEE, WI 53213

THE ACTOR'S SONGBOOK/ MEN'S EDITION

After You Get What You Want You Don't Want It

Words and Music by
IRVING BERLIN

Alabamy Bound

Words by B.G. DESYLVA and BUD GREEN
Music by RAY HENDERSON

Forbidden Fruit
(The Apple Tree)
from *The Apple Tree*

Misterioso

Words by SHELDON HARNICK
Music by JERRY BOCK

11

To Coda ⊕

Need to speed your ed - u - ca - tion, The seeds, in·deed, of all cre-a - tion are
Rel - ish ev -'ry con-ver-sa - tion, Why, you'll be A-dam's in-spi-ra - tion this

here,

Rubato

Why be fool - ish, my dear,

Tempo

Come with me To that tree.

Tpts.
+ Trb.

D. S. al Coda 𝄋

With ev-'ry

All I Really Need Is the Girl

from *Gypsy*

Words by STEPHEN SONDHEIM
Music by JULE STYNE

Moderato (♩ = 92)

TULSA:

Once my ___ clothes were shab-by. Tail-ors ___ called me "cab-bie". So I ___ took a vow, ___ Said, "This bum-'ll be beau Brum-mell." Now I'm ___ smooth and snap-py,

Now my ___ tail- or's hap-py. I'm the ___ cat's me - ow! ___ My

ward - robe is a wow! ___ Pa - ris ___ silk, ___

Har - ris ___ tweed. ___ There's on - ly one thing ___ I

A little slower (♩ = 88)

need. ___ Got my tweed pressed, ___ Got my

best vest, _____ All I need now _____ is the

girl! _____ Got my striped tie, _____ Got my

hopes high, _____ Got the time and the place And I _____ got rhyth - m,

Now all I need's the girl _____ to go with 'em. If she'll _____ just ap -

pear, We'll ___ take this big town ___ for a whirl. _____

_____ And if she'll ___ say, "My dar - ling, I'm yours," I'll throw _

___ a - way ___ my striped tie _____ And my best pressed tweed, _

___ All I real - ly need ___ is the girl!

Amsterdam

from *Jacques Brel is Alive and Well and Living in Paris*

French lyrics and music by JACQUES BREL
English lyrics by MORT SHUMAN and ERIC BLAU

Bachelor's Dance

from *Jacques Brel is Alive and Well and Living in Paris*

French lyrics and music by JACQUES BREL
English lyrics by MORT SHUMAN and ERIC BLAU

Buddy's Blues

from *Follies*

Words and Music by
STEPHEN SONDHEIM

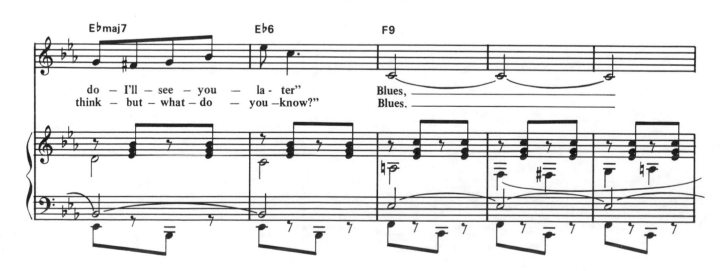

By Myself

from *Between the Devil*

Words by HOWARD DIETZ
Music by ARTHUR SCHWARTZ

The Bulls

from *Jacques Brel is Alive and Well and Living in Paris*

French lyrics and music by JACQUES BREL
English lyrics by MORT SHUMAN and ERIC BLAU

Come With Me

from *The Boys from Syracuse*

Words by LORENZ HART
Music by RICHARD RODGERS

Moderately bright - In 2

Come with me where the food is free, Where the land - lord

nev - er comes near you. Be a guest in a

house of rest, Where the best of fel - lows can cheer

you. There's your own lit-tle room So

cool, not too much light, _____ Where

you're one man for whom No wife waits up at

night. _____ When day ends you have lots of

Much slower - In 2

You nev-er have to fetch the milk Or walk the dog at ear-ly dawn. There's no "get up, you're late for work" While you rest in the pearl-y dawn. You're nev-er bored by pol-i-tics. You're priv-i-leged to miss a row of trag-e-dies by Soph-o-cles And

mf

(sempre stacc.)

39

Del - phi. You snore and swear and stretch and yawn In this, your strict - ly male house. The

on - ly way that sin - ners go to heav - en Is in the jail - house.

Tempo I

Come with me where the food is free, Where the

land - lord nev - er comes near you.

Be a guest in a house of rest, Where the

best of fel - lows can cheer you.

There's your own lit - tle room, So

41

cool, not too much light, _____

Where you're one man for whom No

wife waits up at night. _____

When day ends you have lots of friends Who will

43

Cohen Owes Me Ninety-Seven Dollars

Words and Music by
IRVING BERLIN

45

Dinner for One, Please James

Words and Music by
MICHAEL CARR

Seems my best friend told her of an-oth-er, I had no chance to de-ny,

You know there has nev-er been an-oth-er, Some day she'll find out the lie.

May-be she's not to blame, Leave me with si-lent hours,— No,

don't move her fav-'rite flow-ers, Din-ner for one, please James. James.

Doing the Reactionary

from *Pins and Needles*

Words and Music by
HAROLD ROME

It's dark-er than the dark bot-tom, It rum-bles more than the rum-ba, If you think that the two step got 'em, Just take a look at this num-ber. It's got that cer-tain swing, That makes you want to sing!

The four hun-dred love to sing it_ Ford and_ Mor-gan swing it_ Hand up high_

_ And shake your head___ You'll soon see red do-ing the re - ac-

1.   2.

-tion - a - ry.   So get in it, be - gin it, It's

smart oh so ve - ry to do the re - ac - tion-a - ry!_

Don't Put Your Daughter on the Stage, Mrs. Worthington

Words and Music by
NOËL COWARD

Allegro moderato (*nice and breezy*)

Don't put your daugh-ter on the stage, Mis - sis Worth-ing-ton;

Don't put your daugh-ter on the stage. _____ The pro-

Everybody Loves My Baby (But My Baby Don't Love Nobody But Me)

Words and Music by JACK PALMER
& SPENCER WILLIAMS

With a beat

VERSE

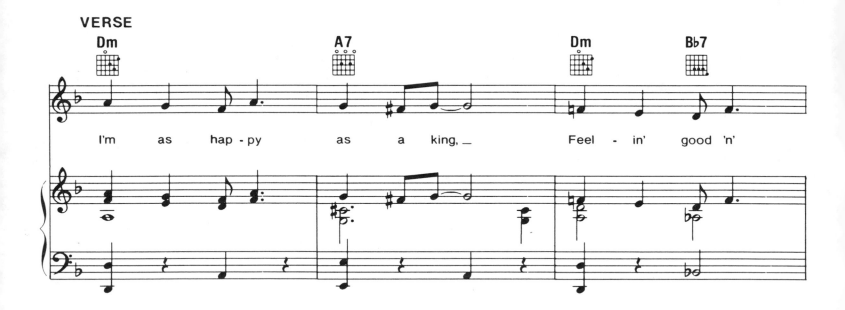

I'm as hap-py as a king, ___ Feel-in' good 'n'

ev-'ry-thing. ___ I'm just like a bird in Spring, ___

MCA music publishing

A Fine Romance

from the film *Swing Time*

Words by DOROTHY FIELDS
Music by JEROME KERN

Andantino moderato *(sung with sarcasm)*

A FINE ro-mance! With
(A) FINE ro-mance! My

no kiss - es! A fine ro-mance, my friend, this is! We
good fel - low! You take ro-mance, I'll take Jel - lo! You're

should be like a cou-ple of hot to - ma-toes, ___ But you're as cold as
calm - er than the seals in the Arc-tic O - cean, ___ At least they flap their

Has Anybody Seen Our Ship?

from *Tonight at 8:30*

Words and Music by
NOËL COWARD

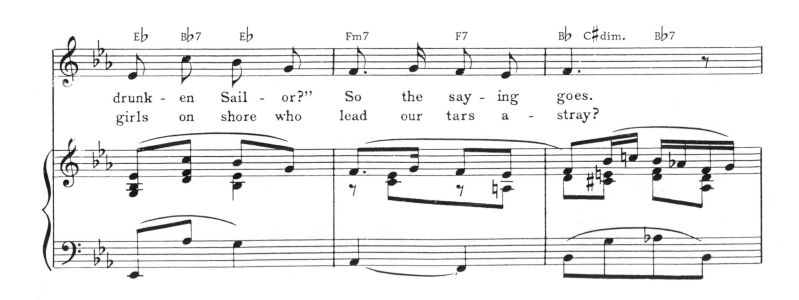

We're not tight but we're none too bright, Great Scott! I don't sup -
What's to be done with the drinks ga - lore That make them pass a -

pose. We've lost our way and we've lost our pay and to
way? We got wet ears from our first five beers, af - ter

make the thing com - plete We've been and gone and
that we lost con - trol And now we find we're

lost the bloom - ing fleet.
up the blink - ing pole.

REFRAIN

Has an-y-bod-y seen our ship, The H. M. S. "Pe-
(Has) an-y-bod-y seen our ship, The H. M. S. "Dis-
(Has) an-y-bod-y seen our ship, The H. M. S. "Sug-

cu - liar." We've been on shore for a month or more And
gust - ing." We've three guns aft and an - oth - er one fore And they've
gest - ive." She sailed a - way a - cross the bay And we

when we see the cap - tain we shall get what for. Heave Ho! me
pro - mised us a fun - nel for the next world war. Heave Ho! me
have - n't had a smell of her since New Year's Day. Heave Ho! me

Heart - ies, Sing Glo - ry Hal - le - lu - jah. A
Heart - ies, The Quart - er deck needs dust - ing. We
Heart - ies, We're get - ting ra - ther res - tive. We

How to Handle a Woman

from *Camelot*

Words by ALAN JAY LERNER
Music by FREDERICK LOEWE

And what of teach-ing me by turn-ing me to an-i-mal and bird, From beav-er to the small-est bob-o-link! I should have had a whirl At chang-ing to a girl, To

learn the way the crea - tures think!

But

was-n't there a night, on a sum-mer long gone by, We pass'd a cou-ple wran-gling a - way;___ And

did I not say, Mer - lyn: What if that chap were I? And did he not give coun-sel and say...___ What

was it now? My mind's a wall._____ Oh, yes! By jove, now I re-call:____

Moderato

How to han-dle a wom-an? There's a way, said the wise old man; A

way known by ev-'ry wom-an Since the whole rig-'ma-role be-gan. Do I

flat-ter her? I begged him an-swer. Do I threat-en or ca-jole or plead? Do I

brood or play the gay ro - manc - er? Said he, smil - ing: No in -

deed. How to han-dle a wom - an? Mark me well, I will tell you,

Sir: The way to han-dle a wom - an Is to love her...

simp - ly love her... Mere - ly love her...

pp

love her... love her. _ten._

optional
ending

(Ponders a moment, then says:) What's wrong, Jenny? Where are you these days? What are you

thinking? I don't understand you. But no matter. Merlyn told me once: Never be too

disturbed if you don't understand what a woman is thinking.

They don't do it often. But what do you do when they are doing it?

I Am What I Am

from *La Cage Aux Folles*

Music and Lyric by
JERRY HERMAN

I Hate You, Darling

from *Let's Face It*

Words and Music by
COLE PORTER

It's true my pet ____ I hate you dar - ling

But don't for - get ____ I hate you dar - ling

And yet I love you so. ____

I

I Wanna Make the World Laugh

from *Mack and Mabel*

Music and Lyric by
JERRY HERMAN

1.3. Heart-break and pas - sion may both be in fash - ion, But
2. Some have a lean - ing for dark, hid - den mean - ing, But

I wan - na make the world laugh. Let
I wan - na make the world laugh. Let

oth - ers do dra - ma of sin and dis - grace While
oth - er di - rec - tors film trag - ic ro - mance, But

I Won't Dance

from the film *Roberta*

Words by OSCAR HAMMERSTEIN II and OTTO HARBACH
Screen Version by DOROTHY FIELDS and JIMMY McHUGH
Music by JEROME KERN

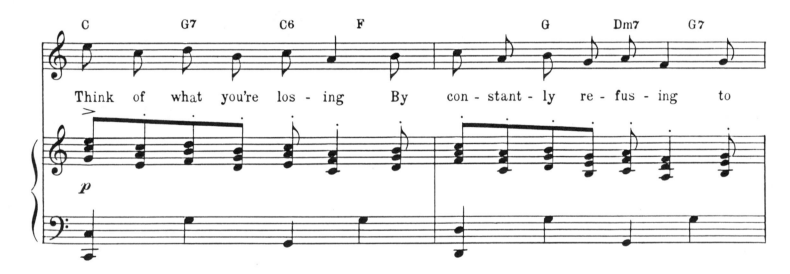

I Won't Send Roses

from *Mack and Mabel*

Music and Lyric by
JERRY HERMAN

Moderately

I won't send ros - es or hold the door;
fran - tic, my tem - per's cross;

I won't re - mem - ber which dress you wore.
With words ro - man - tic I'm at a loss.

My heart is too much in con - trol, the lack of
I'd be the first one to a - gree that I'm pre -

I'll Capture Your Heart Singing

from the film *Holiday Inn*

Words and Music by
IRVING BERLIN

+) *Symbols for Guitar, Chords for Ukulele and Banjo*

I'm Calm

from A Funny Thing Happened on the Way to the Forum

Words and Music by
STEPHEN SONDHEIM

SENEX: *(Shouting)*
Hysterium!

cuse me__ I'm calm, _____ oh, so calm, _____ Oh, so__

Isn't This a Lovely Day
(To Be Caught in the Rain?)

from the film *Top Hat*

Words and Music by
IRVING BERLIN

111

King Herod's Song

from *Jesus Christ Superstar*

Lyrics by TIM RICE
Music by ANDREW LLOYD WEBBER

Moderato, ad lib.

114

118

Lady of the Evening

from *Music Box Revue of 1932*

Words and Music by
IRVING BERLIN

Moderato con molto expressione

Voice

Af - ter the gray of a long drear-y day comes the eve - ning.
Af - ter the sun when its day's work is done comes the eve - ning.

broader

Peace-ful and calm as a shel - ter-ing palm is the eve - ning
Then with the night comes the An - gels who light up the eve - ning

122

123

Leadville Johnny Brown

from *The Unsinkable Molly Brown*

By MEREDITH WILLSON

Spoken: This is my home, here. Leadville! Hell, that's my name, don't you...

Look For Small Pleasures

from *Ben Franklin in Paris*

Music by MARK SANDRICH, JR.
Lyrics by SIDNEY MICHAELS

129

Meditation I

from *Shenandoah*

Lyric by PETER UDELL
Music by GARY GELD

CHARLIE:

They'll say we made life here in Vir-gin-ia, and we owe the com-mon-wealth a thing or two.

(Talks:) Well, if anyone here owes anyone here: - Virginia should be owin' me and . . . . . .you.

Re - mem - ber how it used to be when it was on - ly you and me,

Hook up the mule and the plow. Got a Jen-ny and a Hen-ry An-der-son now; An ap-ple tree with a

Broader *(More deliberate)*   *a tempo*   *rall.*

fruit-ed bow; A lov-in' wife with child a-gain. And I'm think-in' I should sleep with the cow, Mar-tha,

Slowly   **Moderato** *(Slower than before)*

(Spoken:) Now, send for the Doc, no, I best go and bring 'im. Pour me a drink and I'll

yon-der in the barn with the cow.

accel. to - - - - - - - - - - - - - Tempo I   *rit.*   *molto rit.*

drink for joy. *(Sings:)*

Get out the den-im, roll up the ging-ham, name him Ro-bert, he's a boy.

Manhattan Madness

from *Face the Music*

Words and Music by
IRVING BERLIN

Man- hat - tan, Man- hat - tan,

Man-hat - tan, Man -hat - tan, Man- hat - tan mad - ness.

You've got ___ me at last. I'm like a fly up - on a stee-ple watch-ing

Man - hat - tan mad - ness. You've got ___ me at

last. I'm like a fly up - on a stee - ple watch - ing sev - en mil - lion peo - ple do a

rhy - thm _ that draws me with 'em, _ and it's mad. _____

Many Moons Ago

from *Once Upon a Mattress*

Music by MARY RODGERS
Words by MARSHALL BARER

find a lass Who would suit his moth - er's pride. For a prin - cess is a del - i - cate thing, Del - i - cate and dain - ty as a dra - gon fly's wing. You can re - cog - nize a la - dy by her el - e - gant air, But a gen - u - ine prin - cess is ex - ceed - ing - ly rare.

(dolce)

Keep moving

rit.

On a storm-y night, to the cas-tle door, Came the

lass the prince had been wait - ing for. "I'm a prin - cess lost" quoth she. But the

queen was cool and re - mained a - loof And she said: "Per - haps, but she'll

need some proof. I'll pre - pare a test and see. I will

mp

test her thus," the old queen said: I'll put twen-ty down-y mat-tress-

es up-on her bed And be-tween those twen-ty mat-tress-es I'll place a ti-ny pea. If that

pea dis-turbs her slum-ber, then a true prin-cess is she.

a tempo

Now, the bed was soft and ex - treme - ly tall, But the

dain - ty lass did - n't sleep at all. And she told them so next

day. Said the queen: "My dear, if you felt that pea, Then we've

proof e - nough of your roy - al - ty. Let the wed - ding mu - sic

The Modern Major General

from *Pirates of Penzance*

Lyrics by SIR WILLIAM S. GILBERT
Music by SIR ARTHUR SULLIVAN

I am the ve-ry mod-el of a mod-ern Maj-or-Ge-ne-ral; I've

in-for-ma-tion-ve-ge-ta-ble, a-ni-mal, and mi-ne-ral: I know the kings of Eng-land, and I

153

154

In fact, when I know what is meant by "ma - me - lon" and "ra - ve - lin;" When I can tell at sight a Mau - ser ri - fle from a ja - ve - lin; When such af - fairs as sor - ties and sur - pri - ses I'm more wa - ry at; And when I know pre - cise - ly what is

pp slower

157

158

Not My Problem

from *Celebration*

Words by TOM JONES
Music by HARVEY SCHMIDT

view.	If it's so, I'd like	to know: Just what the hell am I sup-posed to

do?	I'd	like	to	see	us	all	be - come	like	saints.	But

since	that	can - not	be,	Then	it's	sim - ply

not	my	pro - o - o - o - blem!

drop-out from hu-man - i - ty. You may think my

mor - als stink. But at least I keep my san-i - ty. I

know the world will soon be go-ing "boom!" De-spite what we may

do. But it's sim - ply not my

Peo-ple die of hun-ger; I re-peat: Not my prob-lem.

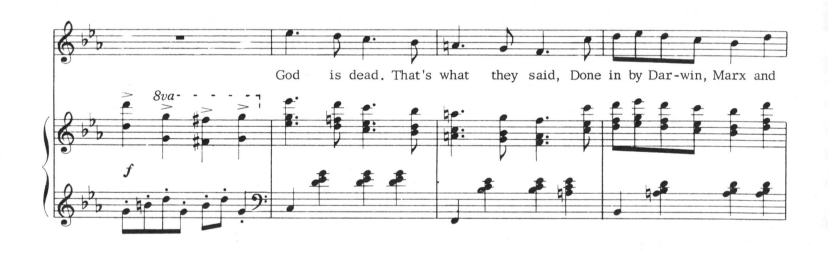

God is dead. That's what they said, Done in by Dar-win, Marx and

Freud. Free are we from de - it-y. Of course, it sort-a leaves a lit-tle

void.   I used to care a - bout my fel-low man.   But

now,   hur-rah, I'm free.   And it's sim - ply

not   my   pro - o ~ o ~ o - blem!

Nina

from *Sigh No More*

Words and Music by
NOËL COWARD

167

She al-so pos-i-tive-ly sta - ted_That she could not a - bide a 'Southern
And then she got more blood-y mind - ed _ And told them where to put_ their 'Trop ic

Moon'.
Palms'.

She said I hate to be pe - dan-tic Bvt I'm driv-en near-ly
And she could not re-frain from say-ing That their i - di-ot-ic

fran-tic When I see that un-ro - man-tic Sy-co-phan-tic lot of sluts.
swaying And those damned 'guitar--ras' play-ing Were an in-sult to her Race.

For-ev-er wrig-gle-ing their guts It drives me ab-so-lute-ly
And that she real-ly could-n't face Such in-ter-na-tion-al dis-

CODA

There surely never could have been a___ More ir-rit-at-ing girl than Ni - na___

They never speak in Ar-gen - ti - na___ Of this de-gen-er-ate 'Bam-bi - na'___

Who had the luck to find ro - mance And res-o-lute-ly wouldn't da - - -

- - - - - - nce! She wouldn't dance!- Hola!!

One For My Baby
(And One More For the Road)

from The Sky's the Limit

Lyric by JOHNNY MERCER
Music by HAROLD ARLEN

173

Once In Love With Amy

from *Where's Charley?*

By FRANK LOESSER

A - my,___ Tear up your list, it's A - my.___

Ply her with bon-bons, po-et-ry and flow-ers, Moon a mil-lion hours___ a-

way.___ You might be quite the fick-le heart-ed ro - ver, So

care - free and bold___ Who loves a girl and la-ter thinks it

Rock-a-Bye Your Baby
With a Dixie Melody

Words by SAM M. LEWIS and JOE YOUNG
Music by JEAN SCHWARTZ

Moderato

Reviewing the Situation

from *Oliver!*

Words and Music by
LIONEL BART

A man's got a heart, has-n't he? Jo-king a-part— has-n't he? And tho'

I'd be the first one to say that I was-n't a saint— I'm

nag at me, The fin-gers she will wag at me, The mon-ey she will take from me, A

Tempo I

mis - er - y, she'll make from me— I think I'd bet-ter think it out a - gain._____

a piacere

—Violin A wife you can keep, an-y-way I'd ra-ther sleep an-y-way, Left with -

Cadenza #1

colla voce

-out an - y - one in the world and I'm start-ing from now—

So

how to win friends and to in-flu-ence peo-ple, so how?_____ I'm re - view-ing_____

𝅗𝅥 = 108

185

Is it such a _____ hu-mi-li - a-tion _____ For a rob-ber to per-form an hon-est job? _____ So a job I'm get-ting poss-ib-ly, I won-der how the boss-'ll be? I won-der if he'll take to me? What bo-nus-es he'll make to me? I'll start at eight, and fin-ish late, At nor-mal rate and all, but wait! I think I'd bet-ter think it out a - gain _____ What

188

Footnote: The lower line of words was used in the original production at The New Theatre, and at this point the scene began to change, Fagin returning to the fireplace to count his money as the revolve took him off.

She Touched Me

from *Drat! the Cat!*

Lyric by IRA LEVIN
Music by MILTON SCHAFER

Steppin' Out With My Baby

from the film *Easter Parade*

Words and Music by
IRVING BERLIN

Sonny Boy

from the film *The Singing Fool*

Words and Music by AL JOLSON, B.G. DESYLVA,
LEW BROWN and RAY HENDERSON

Tschaikowsky

from *Lady in the Dark*

Words by IRA GERSHWIN
Music by KURT WEILL

202

Gla-zou-noff and Cae-sar Cui, Ka - li - ni - koff, Rach - ma - ni - noff, Stra - vin-sky and Gret-

chna-ni-noff, Rum-shin-sky and Rach-ma-ni-noff, I real-ly have to stop, The sub-ject

has been dwelt up-on e-nough! Stra - vin-sky, Gret-chna-ni-noff, Kvo-schin-sky, Rach-

ma-ni-noff! I real-ly have to stop be-cause you all have un-der-gone e-nough!

The Way You Look Tonight

from the film *Swing Time*

Words by DOROTHY FIELDS
Music by JEROME KERN

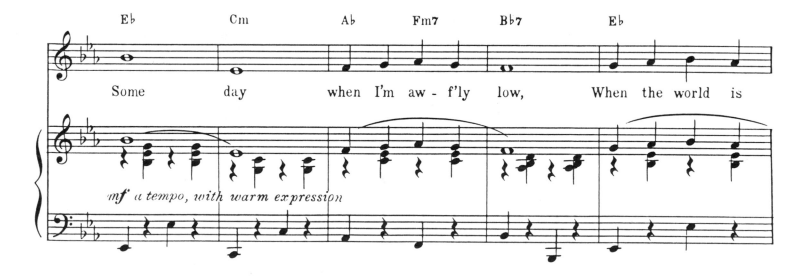

Some day when I'm aw - f'ly low, When the world is

cold, I will feel a glow just think-ing of you

205

What Chance Have I With Love

from *Louisiana Purchase*

Words and Music by
IRVING BERLIN

When I'm Not Near the Girl I Love

from *Finian's Rainbow*

Words by E.Y. HARBURG
Music by BURTON LANE

near. _____ Ev - 'ry femme that flut - ters by me, _____

_____ is a flame that must be fanned. _____ When

I _____ can't fon - dle the hand _____ I'm fond of, I fon - dle the

rall.   *a tempo*

hand at hand. _____ My heart's in a pick - le, it's

con - stant - ly fick - le ___ and not too par - ti - cle, ___ I fear. ___

___ When I'm ___ not near ___ the girl ___ I love, ___ I

rall.

a tempo

love ___ the girl I'm near. ___

What if they're tall and ten - der; What if they're small and

I'm con-fess - ing a con-fes - sion _____ and I hope I'm not ver - bose, _____ When

fan - cy the face I face. _____ For Sha - ron I'm car - in'; _ But

Su - zan I'm choo-sin', _ I'm faith - ful to who - s'n _ is here. _____ When

I'm _ not near _ the girl _ I love, _ I love _ the girl _

_____ I'm _ near.

Where Was I When They Passed Out Luck?

from *Minnie's Boys*

Lyrics by HAL HACKADY
Music by LARRY GROSSMAN

Where I Want to Be

from *Chess*

Words and Music by BENNY ANDERSSON,
TIM RICE and BJORN ULVAEUS

Nearly like a waltz (not too slow); like a music box

ANATOLY:

Who needs a dream?

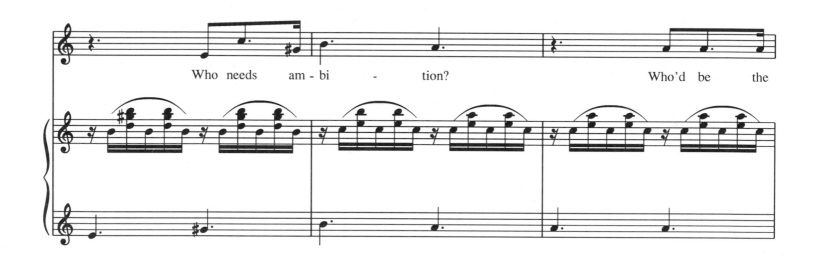

Who needs am - bi - tion? Who'd be the

fool in my po - si - tion?

When the cra - zy wheel slows

down, where will I be?

Back where I start - ed. Don't get me

wrong, I'm not com-plain - ing.

230

231

Who Can I Turn To (When Nobody Needs Me)

from *The Roar of the Greasepaint-The Smell of the Crowd*

Words and Music by LESLIE BRICUSSE
and ANTHONY NEWLEY

Willkommen

from *Cabaret*

Words by FRED EBB
Music by JOHN KANDER

Blei - be, res - te, stay. Will - kom - men, bien - ve - nue,_

wel - come, Im Cab - a - ret, ___ au Cab - a - ret, ___ to Cab - a - ret. ___

Spoken: Meine Dammen und Herren, Mesdames et Messieurs, Ladies and

Gentlemen. Guten Abend. Bon soir. Good evening.

Wie gehts? Comment ça va? Do you feel good?

beautiful.

Even the orchestra

is beautiful.

Ich sa - ge

Will - kom - men, bien - ve - nue, _ wel - come.

Frem - de, é - tran - ger, stran - ger.

Glück - lich, zu se - hen, Je suis en - chan - té. _____

Hap - py to see you, blei - be, res - te, stay.

Will - kom - men, bien - ve - nue, _ wel - come, Im Cab - a - ret, _

_ au Cab - a - ret, _ to Cab - a -

ret.

MUSICAL THEATRE COLLECTIONS
FROM HAL LEONARD

BROADWAY BELTER'S SONGBOOK
A great new collection for women singers. All the songs have been chosen especially for this type of voice, and the ranges and keys have been carefully selected. 30 songs, including: Broadway Baby • The Lady Is A Tramp • Everything's Coming Up Roses • I'd Give My Life To You (*Miss Saigon*) • Cabaret. 176 pages.
_____00311608 ....$16.95

THE SINGER'S MUSICAL THEATRE ANTHOLOGY

The most comprehensive collection of Broadway selections ever organized specifically for the singer. Each of the five volumes contains important songs chosen because of their appropriateness to that particular voice type. All selections are in their authentic form, excerpted from the original vocal scores. The songs in *The Singer's Musical Theatre Anthology*, written by such noted composers as Kurt Weill, Richard Rodgers, Stephen Sondheim, and Jerome Kern, are vocal masterpieces ideal for the auditioning, practicing or performing vocalist.

Soprano
46 songs, including: Where Or When • If I Loved You • Goodnight, My Someone • Smoke Gets In Your Eyes • Barbara Song • and many more.
_____00361071 ....$17.95

Mezzo-Soprano/Alto
40 songs, including: My Funny Valentine • I Love Paris • Don't Cry For Me Argentina • Losing My Mind • Send In The Clowns • and many more.
_____00361072 ....$17.95

Tenor
42 songs, including: Stranger In Paradise • On The Street Where You Live • Younger Than Springtime • Lonely House • Not While I'm Around • and more.
_____00361073 ....$17.95

Baritone/Bass
37 songs, including: If Ever I Would Leave You • September Song • The Impossible Dream • Ol' Man River • Some Enchanted Evening • and more.
_____00361074 ....$17.95

Duets
21 songs, including: Too Many Mornings • We Kiss In A Shadow • People Will Say We're In Love • Bess You Is My Woman • Make Believe • more.
_____00361075 ....$14.95

THE SINGER'S MUSICAL THEATRE ANTHOLOGY VOL. 2
More great theatre songs for singers in a continuation of this highly successful and important series, once again compiled and edited by Richard Walters. As is the case with the first volume, these collections are as valuable to the classical singer as they are to the popular and theatre performer.

Soprano, Volume 2
42 songs, including: All Through The Night • And This Is My Beloved • Vilia • If I Were A Bell • Think Of Me.
_____00747030 ....$18.95

Mezzo-Soprano/Alto, Volume 2
44 songs, including: If He Walked Into My Life • The Party's Over • Johnny One Note • Adalaide's Lament • I Hate Men • I Dreamed A Dream.
_____00747031 ....$18.95

Tenor, Volume 2
46 songs, including: Miracle Of Miracles • Sit Down, You're Rockin' The Boat • Where I Want To Be • Bring Him Home • Music Of The Night.
_____00747032 ....$18.95

Baritone/Bass, Volume 2
44 songs, including: Guido's Song from *Nine* • Bye, Bye Baby • I Won't Send Roses • The Surrey With The Fringe On Top • Once In Love With Amy.
_____00747033 ....$18.95

THE ACTOR'S SONGBOOK
A wonderfully diverse collection of comedy songs, character songs, Vaudeville numbers, dramatic songs, and ballads for the actor who sings. A perfect resource to use for finding an audition song or specialty number. In two editions, one for women, and one for men, with a completely different selection of songs chosen for each edition. Over 50 songs in each book. Women's edition titles include: The Ladies Who Lunch • Cla-wence (Don't Tweat Me So Wough) • Cry Me A River • Shy • The Man That Got Away, and many more. Men's edition includes: Buddy's Blues (from *Follies*) • Doing The Reactionary • How to Handle A Woman • I'm Calm • Reviewing The Situation, many more.
_____00747035 Women's Edition $18.95
_____00747034 Men's Edition $18.95

HL **Hal Leonard Publishing Corporation**
For more information, see your local music dealer, or write to:
P.O. Box 13819 Milwaukee, Wisconsin 53213
Prices, contents and availability subject to change without notice.

KIDS' BROADWAY SONGBOOK
An unprecedented collection of songs that were originally performed by children on the Broadway stage. A terrific and much needed publication for the thousands of children studying voice. Includes 16 songs for boys and girls: Gary, Indiana (*The Music Man*) • Castle On A Cloud (*Les Miserables*) • Where Is Love? (*Oliver!*) • Tomorrow (*Annie*) • and more.
_____00311609 ....$8.95

MUSICAL THEATRE CLASSICS

A fantastic series featuring the best songs from Broadway classics. Collections are organized by voice type and each book includes recorded piano accompaniments on cassette – ideal for practicing. Compiled by Richard Walters, Sue Malmberg, pianist.

Soprano, Volume 1
13 songs, including: Climb Ev'ry Mountain • Falling In Love With Love • Hello, Young Lovers • Smoke Gets In Your Eyes • Wishing You Were Somehow Here Again.
_____00660148 ....$14.95

Soprano, Volume 2
13 more favorites, including: Can't Help Lovin' Dat Man • I Could Have Danced All Night • Show Me • Think Of Me • Till There Was You.
_____00660149 ....$14.95

Mezzo-Soprano/Alto, Volume 1
12 songs, including: Don't Cry For Me Argentina • I Dreamed A Dream • The Lady Is A Tramp • People • and more.
_____00660150 ....$14.95

Mezzo-Soprano/Alto, Volume 2
12 songs, including: Glad To Be Unhappy • Just You Wait • Memory • My Funny Valentine • On My Own • and more.
_____00660151 ....$14.95

Tenor
12 songs, including: All I Need Is A Girl • If You Could See Her • The Music Of The Night • On The Street Where You Live • Younger Than Springtime • and more.
_____00660152 ....$14.95

Baritone/Bass
10 classics, including: If Ever I Would Leave You • If I Loved You • Oh, What A Beautiful Mornin' • Ol' Man River • Try To Remember • and more.
_____00660153 ....$14.95

0693